iScience
Science in the Real World

S0-BAB-607

Pebbles, Sand, and Silt

by Emily Sohn and Diane Bair

NORWOOD HOUSE PRESS
Chicago, Illinois

Norwood House Press
Chicago, Illinois

For information regarding Norwood House Press, please visit our website at
www.norwoodhousepress.com or call 866-565-2900.

Contributor: Edward Rock, Project Content Consultant

Editor: Lauren Dupuis-Perez

Designer: Sara Radka

Fact Checker: Sam Rhodes

Photo Credits in this revised edition include: Getty Images: emholk, 11, iStockphoto, 9, 12, 16, Paul Bradbury, 4, Westend61, 6; Pixabay: Byunilho, background (paper texture), GDJ, background (tech pattern); Shutterstock: Dave Allen Photography, 18, kram9, cover, 1, Microgen, 17

Library of Congress Cataloging-in-Publication Data

Names: Sohn, Emily, author. | Bair, Diane, author. | Sohn, Emily. iScience.
Title: Pebbles, sand, and silt / by Emily Sohn and Diane Bair.
Description: [2019 edition]. | Chicago, Illinois : Norwood House Press, [2019] | Series:
    IScience | Audience: K to grade 3. | Includes bibliographical references and index.
Identifiers: LCCN 2018057547 | ISBN 9781684509676 (hardcover) |
    ISBN 9781684043637 (pbk.) | ISBN 9781684043743 (ebook)
Subjects: LCSH: Soils—Juvenile literature. | Soil science—Juvenile literature.
Classification: LCC S591.3 .P43 2019 | DDC 631.4—dc23
LC record available at https://lccn.loc.gov/2018057547

Hardcover ISBN: 978-1-68450-967-6
Paperback ISBN: 978-1-68404-363-7

Contents

Note to Caregivers:
In this updated and revised iScience series, each book poses many questions to the reader. Some are open ended and ask what the reader thinks. Discuss these questions with your child and guide him or her in thinking through the possible answers and outcomes. There are also questions posed which have a specific answer. Encourage your child to read through the text to determine the correct answer. Most importantly, throughout the book, encourage answers using critical thinking skills and imagination. In the back of the book you will find answers to these questions, along with additional resources to help support you as you share the book with your child.

Words that are **bolded** are defined in the glossary in the back of the book.

Let Your Garden Grow

Have you ever stopped to smell a flower? A healthy flower usually looks and smells beautiful. Plants, such as flowers, need the right kind of **soil** to be healthy. This book will get you digging in the ground. You will learn about soil. And you will learn the best soil to use to grow a perfect garden.

Sprouting Sunflowers

You are a gardener. An elderly
neighbor has hired you. He wants
you to plant a garden. He loves sunflowers.
But he can't do the work himself anymore.

In his garden, you find three piles of soil.

Soil 1: This soil is mostly
small rocks.

Soil 2: This soil is sandy and dry.

Soil 3: This soil is damp and dark.

You want to grow big, healthy sunflower plants.
Which soil would work best?

Discover Activity

Studying Soil

You can use water to learn about soil.

1. Go out to a yard or schoolyard.

2. Use a small shovel or spoon to dig a few scoops of soil.

3. Put the soil in the jar. The jar should be one-quarter full of soil.

4. Add water until the jar is two-thirds full.

5. Put the lid on the jar.

Materials

- 1 hard plastic jar with lid (A clean peanut butter jar would work well; it can be large, medium, or small.)
- 1 small shovel or large spoon
- water
- soil from near your home

◆ After step 5, your jar should look something like this one.

6. Now, shake it up!

7. Wait for 30 minutes.

8. Now look at your jar.

◆ After step 6, your jar should look something like this one.

What is at the bottom? What is near the top?

Look closely at the level of water in the jar now. How does it compare to the amount you put in? How much water do you think the soil soaked up?

The Top Layer

Stand up. Now, look down. You might be on a floor or a sidewalk. But somewhere below you, there is soil.

Some animals live in it. Plants grow in it. Soil is full of life!

Soil may contain bits of broken rock. There are also dead leaves in it.

◆ What can you find in this soil?

What else might you find in soil? Look at the picture for ideas.

◆ Plants would not grow very well in this bed of rocks.

Pebbles, or small, smooth rocks, are common in some soil.

These bits of rock take up space. But they don't offer food for plants.

Are there pebbles in your jar?

Would pebbles be good to have in your sunflower garden? Why or why not?

◆ What happens when you pour water on sand?

All soils are different. Some contain **sand**.

Sand often contains **minerals** that are good for some plants.

But sand is **coarse**. Sandy soil absorbs water quickly. Plants in sandy soil need to be watered often.

Sunflowers need water. Would sand be good to have in your sunflower garden? Why or why not?

Some soil contains **silt**.

Silt is made of tiny bits of rock. These bits are much smaller than pebbles. They are even smaller than pieces of sand.

◆ The soil around a riverbed is often silty.

Silt offers **nutrients** to plants. It also holds water for them.

Many plants grow well in silt. But too much silt can drown plants in water.

Some soil contains **clay**. You may have worked with clay. It is sticky when wet.

Clay can hold food for plants. But it doesn't let much air or water in. Plants need both.

Do you want clay in your garden?

◆ Can you grow a sunflower in clay?

◆ Do you think this soil would hold water well?

Each plant has its own needs. Some need more water than others. Some need loose soil.

But **humus** helps many plants grow well.

Humus contains old, dead bits of plants and animals. It is loose and spongy. It makes soil look dark.

Why might humus be good for your garden?

This chart shows what soil is made of. Plants get some things they need from **organic matter**. This is made of parts of dead animals and plants. They also get nutrients from **inorganic** substances, such as lime, in mineral matter.

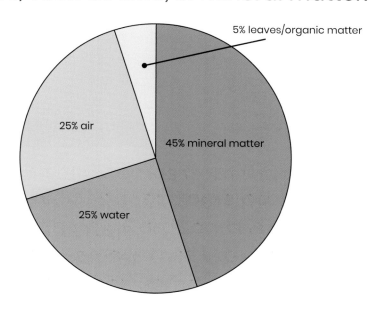

5% leaves/organic matter

25% air

45% mineral matter

25% water

Plants need water, air, and food to grow.

Good soil helps the plants get all of these.

Some soils hold more water. Other soils hold more air. Food supplies can go up and down.

◆ Some creatures living in soil are so small they can only be seen with a microscope.

Did You Know?

Ants, earthworms, and some snakes live in soil. So do some spiders, groundhogs, snails, and slugs.

Some creatures that live in soil are tiny. You have to use a special tool to see them. A microscope or magnifying lens would work for this.

What lives in the soil where you live? How could you find out?

Civil Engineer

Civil engineers help create the places where we walk, drive, and play. They design bridges, roads, and parks. They have to study the ground where something will be built. It is important to make sure the ground is solid and secure.

◆ Civil engineers make sure the ground and water are safe for people to use.

Civil Engineers also design dams and water treatment plants. They make sure we have enough water to drink and that our water is clean.

The Appalachian Mountains are located in the eastern US. They are some of the oldest mountains in the world. Scientists believe they were made more than 500 million years ago. They were once as tall

◆ The Appalachian Mountains stretch nearly 2,000 miles (3,200 kilometers) across the US.

as the Rocky Mountains. But **erosion** made them smaller over time. Erosion gave the Appalachian Mountains a rounded shape.

The Rocky Mountains are located in the western US. They were formed 40 to 70 million years ago. There are many forests on the lower parts of the Rocky Mountains. But the higher parts are very rocky.

The Rocky and Appalachian Mountains are examples of how erosion causes big changes over time.

The Importance of Soil

Plants make Earth look green and pretty. Animals eat them. And so do we. Many plants need soil to grow in. Some can grow on rocks or on other plants.

Some kinds of plants grow only in some parts of the world. Why do you think that is?

◆ Good soil helps this farmer's crops grow. What kinds of plants do you like eating?

Which soil will you choose for your neighbor's garden?

Soil 1:
This soil has lots of pebbles in it. It does not have many nutrients. It does not hold water very well.

Soil 2:
This soil is sandy and dry. An expert could turn it into rich soil. But as it is, sunflowers will not grow well here.

Soil 3:
This soil is damp and dark. It is full of water. It is also full of humus. This one is best for growing sunflowers.

Gardeners often mix soil types, too. They want plants to grow as well as they can.

Beyond the Puzzle

Use what you have learned about soil!

Collect some soil. Put your hands in it. How can you describe it?

Is it dark or light? Is it soft or hard? Are there worms in it?

What happens if you add water? Now, put it in sunlight. How does it change?

Try to start your own garden.

Get some sunflower seeds. Put them in the soil. What do you need to do to help them grow?

What else could you grow in your garden? With the right soil, you could have the best garden in the neighborhood!

Glossary

clay: fine-grained, moist dirt.

coarse: having a rough texture.

erosion: when something is worn away over time by wind, water, and ice.

humus: organic matter from plant or animal remains.

inorganic: describes something that is not made up of living things, such as a rock.

matter: the material that things are made of.

minerals: natural substances found in earth.

nutrients: things plants and animals need for life.

organic: describes something that is made up of living or once living things, such as leaf litter.

pebbles: small, smooth stones.

sand: loose, gritty bits of worn or broken rock.

silt: a material made of fine mineral bits smaller than in sand and larger than in clay.

soil: top layer of our planet, formed from rocks and decaying plants and animals.

Further Reading

Messner, Kate. 2017. *Up in the Garden and Down in the Dirt*. San Francisco, Calif.: Chronicle Books.

Natural Resources Conservation Service. 2018. "Soil Education Grades K–6." United States Department of Agriculture. https://www.nrcs.usda.gov/wps/portal/nrcs/detail/soils/edu/kthru6/.

Tomecek, Steve. 2016. *Dirt*. Washington, DC: National Geographic.

University of Illinois Board of Trustees. 2018. "My First Garden." University of Illinois Extension. https://extension.illinois.edu/firstgarden/.

Additional Notes

The page references below provide answers to questions asked throughout the book. Questions whose answers will vary are not addressed.

Page 8: Depending on the soil, there will be pebbles at the bottom, then sand, then silt. The clay will mostly stay floating in the water.

Page 9: You might find roots, ants, earthworms, or rocks in soil.

Page 10: You wouldn't want too many pebbles in your sunflower garden because there would not be enough food for the plants and water would drain right through.

Page 11: Caption question: The water runs right through the sand.

Page 13: While you wouldn't want your soil to be made up of all clay, some clay is good for retaining nutrients.

Page 14: Humus adds nutrients to the soil. Humus also helps soil retain moisture.

Index